The Sickness Within Me Is Well

Carly Dustman

Presentation by *BookLeaf Publishing*

Web: www.bookleafpub.com

E-mail: info@bookleafpub.com

ISBN: 9789357740333

First edition 2023

ACKNOWLEDGEMENT

Thank you to God & Jesus for looking out for me, keeping my heart well, and for everything I don't realize yet

PREFACE

For anyone that actually reads these prefaces, hello. I usually read them also. I'm not really sure what to say, except that I'm happy to be here, and happy you're here. Having someone to share my words and perspectives with is a lot of fun, so thank you for being my audience. I hope you are doing as well as you can be in this moment. Peace and love be with you I hope. Let's begin the book...

Life and it's many pieces

It's a trip

Around the sun

Every year

Days are long, years fly by

Why did you make me cry
Was that a fly
Did you see the twinkle in their eye

Moments pass
Moments bleed
I kinda don't
Ever want to leave

But only if
You'll stay with me
Cheers to our...

Eternity.

Opening Up

I wanted to make something
I wanted you to see
All the many kinds of things
That flow inside of me

I wanted to make it solid
Something you could read
I wanted to feel the flowing joy
That seeps behind the scenes

My love is mine
But if you feel some too,
That's yours for you to keep

No Money

I write how I feel
It's not always happy
Some days I feel
A little bit crappy

No day is the same
My mood: subject to change
But I'll take a bet
You are the same

Just a bunch of humans
Floating in space (is that true?)
With a lot going on
And a lot we don't say

And just as much
A desire to play
A need to spend the day
In our own way

But what would get done?
Quite a lot I think
But not any of those "productivity" things

The world would collapse

As we know it, at least
We would make art
We would bare our feet

People wouldn't be for sale
We would be free

But all the places we worked
That others liked visiting
Would probably be closed
For money is not a need

How would we spend our time?
Would we think carefully?
Would we see our children
And see the natural need

Create places of fun
Places for free
An abundance of everything
Everyone doing their own thing

And actually time to enjoy it
Time to go see
That new place your neighbor
Opened up joyfully

And maybe more time figuring out
Who we are

As individuals
Not being told to play a part

No need for survival
Cause no one are rivals
Doing everything
For the joy that it brings

Your job would come so naturally
Cause it would be what you wanted
And there would be a need
You created it yourself, joy in the seed

Eggs

I ate some eggs, they tasted fine
Then a person said they were plastic online
Where do these eggs come from
What is true?
I want my own
backyard chicken coop

Patience

Peace
It sounds nice
Peace
I want plenty

Peace...
Do you think
that it would
make me feel
empty?

Peace
I don't know
It sounds pretty nice
I think I could live
On Jesus' advice

This isn't very detailed
It may not have sense
But it's nice to read
Unless you're complacent

"Be renewed by the renewing of your mind"
How do I do that
I think I am fine

Oh yes, but you see
You could be much better
If you could release your vices
Release your tethers

But you have become stuck
Comfy as you seem
Your soul has some very
Different dreams

Find peace, be still
Make peace with your scene
Let your mind wander
Remember your dreams

And always, always
When things get hard
Try to find peace
Don't tear yourself apart

Your time is coming
Your mind will renew
But until that time
Peace is up to you

I Don't Want To Be Like Taylor Swift

You know how a man
says that they love you
And you want to believe them

But I can't handle
The things I'm seein'

I wanted to be done
Found the one I would be with

It never was perfect
Often needed a reset
Some time apart
Back together
The end?

No, you never cheated
I guess, what's the meanin'?
Giving your attention to girls online
Not a chat, but just seeing them

You're open about it all
I wonder if it's my fault
My trust issues are hard

My pulse beating strong

The signs were prodding me
Angel numbers
Her screen tag
In plain sight
Take the call

I heard angel numbers were demonic
Lucifer says take the fall
Give up everything
Pack your stuff, sell it all

Be left with nothing
See who is God
But I know God doesn't care about "things"
He cares about our fall
And if we rise up to him
We're sure to take his call

Patience
Wait a day or two
It might happen much sooner for you
And if you take the time to think
You'll surely outlast the enemies wink

Writing helped me get this out
The emotions, they were such a cloud
I think my trust is even better now

Things are not always how they seem
The enemy plays on you
where you're weak

P.S. I think Taylor Swift is amazing. Alas I can
not want to be like her (seemingly never finding
the right person) and still love her light that
shines so brightly. I've been a fan from the
beginning. And this is just a poem to burn.

Observer of Lives

I like to see how others live
All the many things
I never did

I wonder if I could absorb
My favorite parts
In my mind, they store

Many people I've seen
Are good with plants
I would like to assimilate all that

Another travels on a boat
To be the youngest
To sail the whole world

Oh the courage that would take
But growing up that way
Makes it an easier fate

Yes, there are pieces of others
I would like to save
Copies in my mind, to use myself one day

The greatness I have witnessed

Makes others unknown, more fascinating
What else is there that I would like
That I haven't seen?

My Precious Boy

Your little face
The way you say "eye"
And point to me
When you first awake

Your big blue eyes
Your rosey cheeks
When you smile real big
And I see your tiny teeth

The way you pick up
The words I speak
Learning everything these days
Much more quickly

When you throw a ball
And say "ready"
My heart leaps around
And goes back steady

I hope you will always
Remember these days
When mama and baby
Were learning their way

I take lots of pictures
But it'll never be the same
As seeing you real time
Within my life frame

It will always be good
We'll keep learning new
And enjoy all the time
Spent next to you

No Granted Taken

I am a product of many
Whom came before me
The ones that made the TV
The ones that made...
Well, everything
Lamps, lightbulbs, home heating
Skillets, crackers, pieces for cleaning
Music, speakers, toothbrushes
Pillows, blankets, and there's crutches
Many things
For many needs
All with purpose
Beginning with speed
Because the art of creation
Arises from need
How our ancestors
Wanted things
And went without
But as we see
Many of their ideas
Have been birthed
Into our reality

Thank You
so much

for following
your dreams

Show Me Your History

Art is like history
Taking shape individually
There is not one side to a story
So why is it his
And not told by more, please

Share your stories
His and hers
And in between
Show us yours

Painting, building, poem form
All work is art
But what remains
Is the story that our world contains

So make it last
Make it fast
Make it sloppy
Make it crass

Maybe it's not his at all
But "Hi Story!"
Open to all

Growth takes time, and a lot of repetition

Being a mom
It's amazing
Especially when I first held
This person my body had been making

I'll never forget
How odd it was
To be so surprised
To feel your warmth

What was I expecting?
I'd never done it before
But when they laid you on me
The realness set in

Fast forward a year
You do so many things now
It's really amazing
Because that's not how you started out

I guess it's a reminder
To begin somewhere
When you want to do something
You'll always find a way

Another thing is
The way mothers are treated
Maybe it's in my head, maybe just the media
But it makes me really sad
To think we aren't appreciated
That our time spent with our babies
Is not valued, seen how it is
All that women do
Shouldn't make men feel depreciated
It can be really hard
Doing so much work
Being a mom is not one job
It's laundry, dishes, dinner, cleaning, gardening,
fixing, making, all while also taking care of a
baby
And we do it all, mostly without complaining
So lend a hand when you can
Every little bit helps
And makes us feel not alone
With the list of chores
For maintaining what we've built

Preferred Daydreams

What I like to daydream of
Is laying in the grass
But doing it in real life
The bugs might bite my ass

So I dream of laying in the grass
Somewhere far away
Soaking in the lovely rays
Of sunshine in the day

Another thing I like to imagine
Is riding with a gypsy family
Traveling in a wagon
I'm not sure how I found them
But they let me tag along
And I learn all kinds of things
About surviving and their songs

The Game We're All Playing

It's been made more clear to me
The Division, the Separating
The attempts to make God angry
The Devil's works, versus the Lord's

I was pondering and I don't believe
The Lord made up any kind of disease
But if he did, he really made it clear
That all of the ingredients to heal were here

Not made by someone I do not know
But right from the earth
Where you can see it grow

This is not to cause fear or freak you out
Many can be trusted
And our bodies are stout
It's up to you to believe or doubt

It takes courage to believe
In things we can't see
But we do it all the time
You don't even know me
But you feel something...?

This doesn't mean
I want to leave the Devil out
I think he's just angry
Because he wants his own clout

God made him precious
The brightest angel of all
But this is god's way of saying
He doesn't hate you at all

I'm wondering now about the holy ghost
The Father and the Son
We already know
But the third spot is a ghost
Cause you haven't really shown
UP in your spot, Devil, come on

Love is All there is

From this side of the fence

Let
  It
    Sink
      In

Can't imagine it?
That's a tragedy

Set yourself free
You don't have to be who you were
A new moment is waiting
Shake off the fur

Not Spoiled

I would say I was blessed
But I couldn't accept it
They gave me the very best
I couldn't accept it

So I laid them to rest
Went on my way
Rebelled against them

I always wanted to give my best
Not have it given to me
But I guess I was blind
Because there is mutuality

Channeling

Sometimes it seems like
That's what I do
Writing about a life
That to my own, isn't true

Communicating between worlds
In the middle of a few
The ones that really matter
Cause it all begins with them

A spiritual world
With physical linked in
Trying to have peace
Seep to the other side of the fence

Cause if everything is right with you
I think for us all it will sink in
Shit rolls downhill
But what if it wasn't shit

Travel

It looks great in my mind
But I don't just appear
At a seaside cliff in Ireland
Except between my ears

There's travel involved
By plane, train, or car
A bus or a shuttle
Could get you pretty far

If you want to go somewhere
I guess it's pretty clear
There's travel involved
To get from there to here

Apologize

I wanted to make better poems
But life got in the way
Took on this challenge
A poem everyday

The last day approaching
Finish up or lose what you paid
So I did my best
To work with the restraints

I hope it has been enjoyable
I hope it has made you think
Don't believe all you hear
And for now I must leave

www.ingramcontent.com/pod-product-compliance
Lightning Source LLC
LaVergne TN
LVHW010953200726

843509LV00013B/2403